Everlasting Quail

Everlasting Quail

Sam Witt

· for The Bridge -
Library -
February 25 2009
Charlottesville VA

Middlebury College Press
Published by University Press of New England
HANOVER AND LONDON

Middlebury College Press
Published by University Press of New England,
Hanover, NH 03755

© 2001 by Sam Witt
Printed in the United States of America
Book design by Dean Bornstein

Library of Congress Cataloging-in-Publication Data

Witt, Sam, 1970-
 Everlasting quail / Sam Witt.
    p. cm.
 ISBN 1-58465-120-2 (cloth : alk. paper) — ISBN 1-58465-121-0 (paper :
alk. paper)
 I. Title.
 PS3573.I9159 E9159 2001
 811'.6 — dc21   00-012777

I too was not, nor my understanding that resolves things out of the images of the senses. I was not the one who saw, but only seeing. And what I saw were not things . . . but only colours. And I too was coloured into this landscape.

— Walter Benjamin, *Dialogue on the Rainbow*

Table of Contents

PART THREE

Acknowledgments

Grateful acknowledgment is made to the editors and readers of the following journals in which these poems originally appeared: *Epoch*: "Her Blue Dress"; *Fish Drum*: "Rhapsody in Crisper Green"; *Volt*: "The Fine Art of the Skull" and "Song of the Daughter"; *Colorado Review*: "Everlasting Quail"; *Quarterly West*: "Theories of Color — A Dialogue in the Rainbow"; *Phoebe*: "Waterfowl Descending"; *Fence*: "Americana 2"; *Poetrymagazine.com*: "Late Snow Falling," "Rhapsody in Crisper Green," and "From a Book of the Dead"; *Shampoo.com*: "A Face in the Hospital Bar"; *Poetry Flash*: "And of the Nature of the Sea Which in Ebbing and Flowing Seemes to Observe so Just a Dance, and Yet Understands No Musicke". In addition, I wish to thank Kevin Prufer, editor of *American Poets Born After 1960*, (Southern Illinois University Press), 2000, in which the following poems appeared: "Americana 1"; "Waterfowl Descending," "Michael Masse," and "Everlasting Quail."

I would like to thank the following people for their support during the writing of this manuscript: Carol Frost, for picking the manuscript; Michael Collier, Ian Pounds, and Ellen Wicklum, for helping to see it through publication; and all others who helped me during its composition, including Marvin Bell, Jorie Graham, Sean Durkin, Garrett Scott, Tessa Rumsey, Tom Thompson, Michael Brendsel, Robert Hedin, Rachel Zucker, Charles Wright, Rita Dove, George Garrett, Debra Nystrom, Reginald Shepherd, Eric "Max" Leach, Jim Willingham, Jim Galvin, Kerry Shawn Keys, John Isles, Ellen Sharp, Paul Holtz, Aaron Cohen, David Bromige, David Reid, Jayne L. Walker, Greg Orr, Timothy Liu, Jane Mead, Joyce Jenkins, and, especially, Bruce March, Anthony McCann, and D. A. Powell, without whose support, close readings, and sense of humor this book could not have been written.

Last, and most of all, I would like to thank my family: Sam Witt, Sally Witt, and Clay Witt.

Everlasting Quail

The Mortality Tree

Whispering in the ghosts of nerves —
mulberry, blood-orange, apple — my people
spreads its loving fingers

like a shady disease. Long, petrified roots
like my loving fingers touch the dead.
The fruit falls excessively with a human thump:

under the spreading chestnut tree
I kissed you and you kissed me

Bruised and hobbling, Uncle Drunk,
go on looking for your glass leg. Great Auntie Nothing,
honey that won't wash off,

embroidering a quiet, see-through shawl:

don't ask for a kiss. You've been breathing again
and you smell like a skunk's dream:

under the wasted chestnut tree,
the girl I love is trapped in 1933

and I call it a game
the way her shadowy flower neglects to open —
petal by petal swallowing itself,

stem and all, a laughing rose; a root,
spreading its love-shades inward; a tree at last,
branchless and leafless and curled:

a magnificent butterfly folding back to its silk pouch,
O people, now and forever amen.

PART ONE

Rhapsody in Crisper Green

To hunger in the bleached light of the refrigerator,
ammonia-splash, what roots are disappearing, I can hear
a wind whistling in your molar, Uncle Bitch, Honeycow,
Harness: to breathe, to fledge, to bird, by oneself or in
company. With my face like a fingerprint in gunpowder —
a hair, longing down from the immaculate sky,
sun-strand —

I'm caught singing *sackcloth and ash, sackcloth and ash*;
you are the sun's brief linen, undergarmented in the
kitchen, discarded on the parquet.

Caught singing *Uncle*, colorful sleeve of a fisherman's
sweater, devoured like tongue in the crisper's pregnance,
the colors, collapsing in my hands.

To go out like the sun, with a laugh.

To chuckle a downpour like the ice-maker.

                              I am spending my eyelids
numerously in this harmless rain, lips on a cigarette,
spending these notes in your earless ear. I can smell your
thirst taking me apart nerve-wise, Uncle, even your slightest
gesture carries the scent of a summer rain . . .

I fledge myself to thee, sang the worm, Uncle We, milk
of furtive days, Uncle Years, and years of it, steady drip
of the faucet eating away the morning (hang on;) to pig,
to bristle like a hairbrush, to root; it's you, it's me,
wrist me beyond the shadow of a shadow,

to cipher the fingerprints of the lost, their breathing
a constant mumble of freon; mine, O seeker of lost hordes,
where is the real person in all of this.

(No, only the dust in the corner is 80% skin.
It's dry, like desert soup; Uncle, it's tough trying to
breathe for the world in these silent ditches, Uncle,
in the trees.)

                                    I have slept so long
in the sun, my brain has roasted through, an eggplant,
splitting at the seams, needless as traffic and sizzling,
(hang on . . .)

No, it's only the refrigerator belt, starting up its steady song
to the leftovers, feeding off my breasts.
Dear Auntie Me, I am hungry for pain this morning,
my glaucous sins, brutal and glutinous as the sky.
O preserve me in Uncle Salt, Uncle Sated, make love
to my blue, blue eyes, to the gunmetal blue,
wherefore it hurts to stare.

                        Don't make tea from my eyelids.

To have a child, to have not a child, childless behind
the Quiktrip by the dumpster, the gulls widowing a circle
in the sky, riffing off our heat, about to snap us into sleep,

to rip myself open and let some blue squeak in, some sky,
to survive.

Don't exhaust my fingerprints on all the ice-cubes.
Don't dissect my throat.

If I want to lie
here in the personal dark and touch myself, what's it to you,
smiling so happily in the dawn's shredded light?

(And you dare call yourself yesterday?)

(And you dare call yourself green?)

Not the ice-cream, not the broccoli, not your pickled eggs.
Not last week's Shepherd's Pie. Not the person behind me,
who laughs in a whisper, and fades.

The Nap

for Beverley Gordon Shepherd Crenshaw,
1906 – 1997

Then the sunshine, with its straightrazor
resting gently against her neck —

              a strangling in a distant yard,
just back of her throat,

15 minutes before sundown,

              the loose wattle of a waterhen
I once held

        between finger and thumb . . .

Can't hardly breathe it's so hot.

        The boy kept smelling a shadow of rain:

turnip greens, simmering downstairs
in molasses and vinegar:

        her slip,

damp from the john   [half of you no longer moves]
hung over a chair beside me.

Fingering that yellowed satin so softly,

        I almost wasn't there, so softly with each intake of air,

and all those decades of nakedness
spayed beneath the sheets:

        dip of a collarbone:

a clavicle half-buried:

        [where is the heft of your chest now]

the blue vein   rooted in sunshine and milky flesh,
a tulip sunk in a glass bowl of motor oil.

Everything I didn't know about us
distilled into the air —
                        dirty bathwater. Day's end,

widowing a waterdrop into copper
                                as it fell from the faucet
into one of Minerva's painted
drinking glasses.

Head shored to one side, wasn't it almost mine, lower lip agape,

feasting on a turned-up smile ... almost *him*, aren't I,
drinking quietly in the next room, placing

a moth's wing in the album
where an upside down airplane stamp
should be   [am I not —

                    no   no   not a starling

apant on the cold   cold floor
                        a wing-shadow, passing across your belly,

a stirpe of dust-motes decirculating?
                    no   little thing

asleep in your watching by the bed
                        in the shadow-pulse

of my temple:]

                    in my fear
[where is your body]   my fear

9

_____of touching her, of diminishing
into the parquet floor,

black-and-white, diminished into a devolving light:

[bloodclot   a certain thinking   thought
hemisphered   a passing through
did you smell
the 13 copper wires melted together
in the brain

sing me back into that short circuit of breathing —]

if I reached out my finger and touched her nape but no,

[the nape
of your neck will never be the same
fissioning into blue deltas   meaning
drift and dissolve   blue radiance of capillaries
blue mud pulled from a creekshelf
meaning   *hush child*
a touched bell

singing of tonguelessness   minute
electrical current purring   thromboning through you
flicker of decay   us   ]

Then a finger,
lightly brushing the pressure point of her temple —

then the boy waking, and withdrawing his hand,
a bump and scuff of clockweights

one day I shall visit you
wearing the light's bronzed slippers   And woke.

Zeromass   Erozmass

Zeromass	Erozmass
Of shine damply	*salted*
In a dirty	*lukewarmth in me*
Tea-stained	*is it*
Slipcase	*dark matter*
By my left cheek	*clean through me*
Diasporous light	*cleave*
O warm	*(her bleached hair)*
Saltwater	*through me*
(Now evaporated)	*wherethrough*
Ago	*or was*
2:59 pm	*& please*
She stood over me	*that thumps the glass*
Parlorsofa	*in my sleep?*
Napquiet	*'suresuresuresuresure'*
Will you please	*by light*
This headache	*that streams*
A rubber fleet	*of a dog's stomach*
The size	*fleshsong*
Of a dog's stomach	*dissects my inner eye?*
In her hand	*'just a bird'*
Will you please	*dysmantled*
In each auscultation	*that I listen*
That listened	*called seconds*
To my small form	*through the bay window*
Ruptures from	*I stream*
An upright clock	*Will you please*
'Lift your legs'	*please fleshsong*
Make this headache	*sleep a dyssolved*

Go away?   *headache*
Clockweights bumping   *travelthrough*
In a tall wardrobe   *of the clock*
Black suit   *'just a dragonfly'*
Of seconds within   *that taps the window*
Disintegrated to a dry   *dysintegrated*
Defabricant rot   *make it go away?*

Dysdysdys   the clock's internals whirred: *dysdis int*
Through me please when you lift Gran the rubber tummy
4 corners a kid could hide in *intintint* by the grate

3 times strikes its hour
the vibrance through the back of my head

I have *desolation* illness   ante-sound
Of sunlight   ticking *my* dyslodged
HEARTAWAY
streams through me   *implanted* in the *sofa*
through a *crack*
in *sun-roasted* drapes   midday *light*
tarnished underface *of* a blazing *mirror*
This headache *of* dyssipating mercury
Black-haired chemical wash *called* me
on *the* parlor wall   *take* my gaze
where the heat *slept*
in your *small* form
before *I* called out   *but* now
I *can* see through *the* wallmirror
into *that* small room
behind my head
Consumes the oxygen
in that silver *reflected* tomb

just *behind* my eye *now*
you sleep
where the ticking *devours* itself but *then*
her cold amniotics
rushed downward
through *a* rubber tube
'*keep* still now'
'*Or* I'll slap *your* face'
Into & *through* me
cold *tears* uprushed me   *a* saltbreeze
Of *human* weight that *swings*
between the *clock's*
thin mahogany *walls*
3:01
Sings *a* last shred   *Of* silence
Implanted *just* above my *carceral* eye
just *above* its desolation *tick* & dissolving
to a *smell* of lemons
I lie still
Flows through me
a petri-dish of *human* dust
Please   *the* rooms
are *pregnant* with us
pregnant with our *impermanence*
Music of *being* lifted still   *Please*
I lie *still*   this notch
after notch   in *my* wooden ear
a bright heavy *murmur*   if I
blots me downward   *rise*
& her *zero-mass*
applumedwashed*through*

will *you* pleasShhhrise   *away*
this particulate *headache*
clockchair*wall*
go away?
'*suresuresuresure*'
to warm *through* me   rise?
Desolation Of My Heartaway Streams

Implanted Sofa Crack Sun-roasted Light Of Mirror

Of Black-haired The Take Where Slept Small I But

Can That Consumes In Reflected Behind Now

Where Devours Then Her Rushed A Keep Or Your

Just Carceral Above Smell I Flows

A Human The Pregnant Pregnant Impermanence Being Please
Rise   Zero   Mass   Through

You   Wall

Michael Masse

Blue thigh of daybreak, sweetened, fall apart —
my fourteenth year: a drop of oil on his thigh.
I know that room like the back of my heart,
aquarium blue: subcutaneous: a lambent sigh. . .

September: sleeve of drowsy hornets: the fallen pear glutted with
    blood:
I did not warm myself over that heat.

One man's soft spot is another man's temple.
Fifteen, sixteen, I'm silver-tongued — "Ssshhh . . . they'll hear."
And swallowing his white hair in headlight, simple,
one man's juiced footprints are my rotting pear.

Gallowgrass, nodding off outside in the wind — Michael, I said —
face of wept meat —

A taper, dripping tallow on my gut.
A swallow's feather curling into smoke,
and breath — for we are the very food of light —
a fingery gaze, a breeze that scalds the lake.

And your flesh? The tiny bloodrose where his lips withdrew.
And your kiss?

A dolphin's back that lifts me in a dive:
I fall into that softening and live.

Late Snow Falling

1.

I don't care that happiness falls this way,

gone tomorrow, half a life
and rising.
Or that my fingertips have let go their sense
most trippingly...

                   Pillows, endless pillows — the defrocked air
filling a cheapened grave.

                       Where should I have lain.
Where should I have stained these perfect sheets,

O me, slipcase
             of pulverized glass, frozen lipmarks
fossilizing each surface

and the slick branches hum like tuning-forks.
Early March —
               bearfat,
layered overhead to keep us cold — ice-slurried river — *seeing*,
lodged like glittering windows.

(Half my life has passed, once defibrillated, half a lungful and rising,

I don't care that we decompose
into this distally radiated clean:)
                   imped to the air;

call me Featherhead,
just a flash in the pants

16

and falling —

2.

I shimmy my way, I whisker like a catfish
through the distressed air —

3.

The river being bodiless beneath its scarred ice
                    (*last night I dreamt a slaughtered pony in the river —*)

Lord, the river bleeds through its cracked skin like my breathing.
                    Tendon-ripple, swollen and red.

Turned in the leafrot, shouldering a snowgrowth
                    into these lifted currents and away.

Dipped my wrist in the water. Felt Your icy pull. Wanted to sleep
                    under Your white hair.
                    I am nothing more than Your veins, Lord.

          I am dusting your branches
          in an emptied white, Lord
          (*for we are glue,*)

and my heat:
                    dusted tonight in its juiced timbre

and hum: a chip of snow
                    clutched in Your eyelashes,

a handful of empty syllables under Your breath,
                    ankle into the river,

calf, hip . . .

Beverley

My thoughts mean less and less,
posted to me from a hospital bed, a-hush in a wave of ether and
    dust,

posted to this room full of candlelight.

Thinking: townlights do not wholly flicker as they should,

as they did four decades ago
with each electric shock they sent through you,

(four electrodes, fixed to your temples, and wrists,)
thinking *pain defeating*.

And no more will you suffer and move as I do tonight,

like all of us born from the chamber of a gun, trigger-finger
against the tongue, thinking:

suffer no more in the black belly of the retina —
meadow in my eye — frost,

chiseling away the window — your face: *pain*

defeating: the crystalline cherry of your brain eaten away

with each slow stroke of candlelight — when I stand up in the wind,
music is the death of me,

I am the death of music, the carcass
of a guitar, and sing, and sing...

you are the burned child without scars
sucking on a chunk of ice.

I am that dollop of life on your tongue, that daughter,
widowed to a dying mind,

as slowly — swatch of green, with your bright, empty curls,

your sack of corroded pennies —
slowly the lights flickered, the candleflame flickers,

I hack my way through the pasture-dark tonight
with each throw of the switch, I follow it until I can feel you,

deep as a bell sounding in a cow's rusted ear,
tethered as I am to that electric sobbing.

(And your tears mean a little less,
puncturing the air from birdcall to birdcall,

lugubrious, glycerinated, some shapeless clepsiderata.)
The signatures of squirrel's feet are disquieting tonight,

coming through the sloped ceiling, a human whisper:
I am not in a meadow, my life

piled in the corner with the dehydrated milk.
(And my thoughts mean a little less,

pinned to each finger, one, two, three . . .)

Yesterday I was a shetland pony, so small
I fit into your pocket of crumbling sugar.

(for daylight has hidden its scraps beneath my skin.)
Yesterday, the sun was a mouthful of blood, falling.

"That's my wound," I thought,
"the shot I fired. There's a bullet in here."

Americana 1

Onely in thy wig, Sister, does the sky clear —

hush of a June shower, lashed flesh of a sapling that bleeds the sky

to the color of bathwater, a thin dish of sunset
for tall colors, like *us*, to sip.

On Tuesdays, like today, I can only perform simple tasks.
Listening to squirrels build a lovely nest between the walls,

the human scamper of those tiny, whispering feet.

Pulling dark, Sister, the powdered hair over my poor,
my broken crown on the front stoop,

I have an earwig that sings, *speake, Sister, that I may know thee*...

As station wagons pass me by, I am too lazy to eat,
blue-eyd & forgotten,

fingering the oversized marshmallow peanuts from certain truck-
stops,
a coward to my own bald thoughts.

On Tuesday I swallowed a monstrous mouthful of bathwater,
& forgot.

Forgot my slender hair washing in the wind.

For nine long years behind smokd glass I slept, my throte
of silver embalmd,

Nine long months enwrappd in your fleckd voice, Sister, singing:
sleep,

("sleep in a grainfield on your feet, & the sweep of the grain

shall be a great river overspilling its banks, a woman, brother, you
    & I,
letting our long hair down,

speaking in many soft fingers to the wind — ") Lethe-sister,
I have my life to drink.

I do not belong here, I belong everywhere, a tiny speechless
pinwheel of sparks

that hanged in the sky, unchanged & changing, of acetylene
that cries so brightly in the sun:

("You must not speak of the long hairs that sufferd through us —")
its long, tired tail of frozen gas in the year of Visitation

was of a dull, languid color, very heavy, and slow,
dragged across the sky (& blue,) nodding off into our long wake,

savage & lean, Sister, in my hungry cry,

a human hair borne through the blue, a hairbell, playd out in the
    wind.

I *am* the miracle fabric, that flash
when you flipped your hair in the sunshine ages ago,

(Onely you know it's a wig) & fade fast, (it's my life,) shorne away,
stroked by tired fingers now on my knees,

(You must not pet the wigs when I smell candle wax on an empty
    stair)
Thy empty face, hung with starres now, (you must not sell your
    hair) & frozen dewe,

on the First and Last Day, Sister,
(O weave me a shirt of that black, black hair that I may live)

when I spilled from myself & away.

Why I Hate the King

Yesterday, I snapped my silk suspenders
over my shoulders and thought about Charles I,
beheaded rather than hanged, "to spare him
the indignity of ejaculating in public."
Every morning I try to save myself from this.

I'm thinking of a bearded lady as the axe falls.
I'm thinking of autumn pears, already
nailed to the ground in the backyard, already covered
by the silver shawl of my widowed season. It's a dignity
we'd save ourselves from everyday, if only we could.

Americana 2

Mother, I know your kitchen's nothing like mine,
with its flawless faucet and its limeguarded sink.
With a wingnut in my fist, I stumble
into the kitchen, it's telling me something, I think:
hatchling, she says, the sun swallowing itself, can't see . . .
I want to know the landscape between these two rooms, the
    stumble
between two walls.
Those aren't really birdcries you hear son
but chips of wet porcelain
I'm scouring with my fingers.
Those aren't really birthwaters, the sink
stained with our fingercuts.
This morning I was afraid to speak for once — wingnut, judah,
birdcall, driblet, joy, (aren't the birds lovely,)
this morning my mother calls to tell me I have a nice ass.
I want to hear those swallows
sinkholing the air with their hunger cries:
we delight in the closing of our eyes
into the green shadows of quince fruit,
she calls to tell me
there's more to life than a piece of ass,
it's sunset, it's dawn, go outside, but I don't,
I can't sleep,
a cloud stuffed into trousers, a stumble
between two eyes,
and through thee darkness, mother, hath fallen on mine eyes:
the thumbprints of two dead stars,

a hoarze wheeze, a whisper,
quailed to the breezy silences: *I love you, winglet.*
I'm eating your green,
I'm rubbing you between my fingers,
she pulls the words out of me,
pulls the teath out of me, my bread tastes of stone.
She tells me that pain is my favorite word, the ear
perfected in its joy, deaf, the birds perfected,
unheard, hatched into their cries:
we are thousands, unrelated, unweighting the branch.
Joy in the spleen, pickled, jarred; joy in the liverdust
scattered through a sifter, in my troubled skin,
in the dust of moder's teeth,
I happily shine the morning, the emptiness
where once your spleen
was plugged and warm. The cold spot,
just under an infant's tongue,
spreading throughout his entire body until he's still
from that one blue touch of —
is it joy? A breeze stumbles me through the door —
moeder, I embrace the handkerchief soaked in bile,
I embrace the nail boiling in your happiness,
she puts my finger in her mouth, she puts my voice
in her mouth, each of her surfaces suckles the touch
out of my fingertips, linoleum and tile.
"There's more," she whispers.
She wills the sun down
and hides it in the leaves,
it's dawn, dissolved into a fine paste between my eyes.
She leans into me, into the cranial wrinkle
in my stomach, (I have to piss, I have to shit)

"taste your food," she says. I sing.
I do not sing. I sing the milk
and there is no song, without thread and clothed,
I'm carrying an empty plate. I swallow.
Taste your food, judasberry. Hang from the Elder tree.
Float face down in the bathwater,
she whispered,
once a room held me, a stutter
between two walls, motherspace, suckle,
what passes through me,
O get it up for your food.

The Fine Art of the Skull

Every day I look into my mother's eyes
I have not seen my mother's eyes in a long long time
I find that her eyes are not real enough

who never looked through another's eyes

& for a short while my hands grow empty.
Mother, your daughter will be a green thread;
look into your hands, worm,

hell was a green place: a green thought.
Candlelight scribbling itself on the walls, orange, pigs. A scream
like candlelight scribbling itself into my head.

In the cracks today I was so certain;
in the spaces that leave a man reading in a green wood,
ear-stopped, his eyes are tunneling his face of blue streams,

he carves himself into the silences, lighting a candle,
it's warm: his eyes are the eyelets of an immaculate shoe.
The candle plants shoots in his side. What's a window

doing out here? Committing surgery scalpels
on the air's *ribcage*, (O bless me:) wanted to destroy the line.
Wanted nightingale & glassy air: spinelit, eyehole,

that's my field, tongueling. Wanted my breeze swollen.
Swallowed the hero's silverfish, *drowned, my daughter*: a cow's
    side, slapped
into the memory of meat, the memory of my hair burning,
    the man

in the wood can't quite bring her back,
fat stitched to a spine, can't quite say *borrow, entrail, breeze* . . .
I took a green to my hero, swallowed, wanted, black:

I have slept in the heat of the sun. The hero's
green, & soft, & drowned, who would not breathe,
I hear his bubbles exhausting through my nose,

father, featherlisp, troubled skin, teeth,
fall into mine eyes, which lead nowhere, which are hollow,
(I shine,) which hollow, which graft, which sieve.

Today the wind was so alone
it called my name: *samuel brown witt is here.*
But how do I know that isn't my own head, lolling

before me on a stalk, all factory,
starthirsty, all the right vibrations of an empty place,
still greenly, the silence that voices thee —

mother, I shall set a burning candle in your inner thigh.
The airdust is my shepherd, is my stomach, is my hell;
it's not a question, hairlip, spider, just two eyes —

dust of a swallow's speckled eggshell,
I was born to sleep, a gift of green tongues: *awake*,
among blades of grass I snuffed out, dissolving into this field,

I dozed by the lip of a scalding lake,
please, hell was a green place, damp hair underfoot
but I forgot, & woke up just now in the scrape

of a shovel, glyphed to an eyelid, the light
silkworming its way through my pores, O flutter,
nothing is ever the same, the cat's got my guts,

my green hair, my foetal skull:
nine seconds, nine months — the squirrels have carried away my
   tongue.
See, I have these eyes, pecked away by grackles,

this morning I swallowed spiders by their veins,
picked from the plied siding; tethered to that darkness, I braille
   the air made dumb:
a man lights his hair on fire, I am feathered to this pain —

I died laughing I fear, and now I can't stop.

A man lights his hell on fire in a green living room
because it burns. It is really a forest, please,
where are the birds — trill, whistle, & loom.

I died laughing I fear . . . Once I saw a line of burning trees
& I said *daddy, darkly,* they were children
set on fire, turning in place in the bright space of leaves.

They were a beautiful hair. They were burn.

PART TWO

A Face in the Hospital Bar

near SF General

Between my ½ and the condom dispenser,
bolted to the wall; here, where **NEW AND EXCITING SAVAGE BLISS**
stands in its fragility, a smudged human forehead shape
just barely reflected in the rippled epiderm of tinfoil
behind the gin bottles and empty glasses,

between my ½ and my ½ ,
I wear my face proudly like a surgical instrument,

an X scratched into plaster, a room exchanging its fluids with mine,
when I drink, its missing face with mine, between my ½
and this portal, which dissolves in me, sing in me, Stoma,
Sing in me repeated a dysfigured mouth:
This is anybody else in the form of your father.

A wall streaked with grease crayon, and ballpoint pen.
I swallow rather than speaking,
swallow matchflames one by one,
and the moment extracted from my mouth
like a little person, torn between the light

into this too too general amnesia to stand in this space,
where I find myself moving without moving:
Wearing a room that inhabits me
just to gestate its sunshine
through the streaked, plastic window as a moment of separation

from the dimness, suddenly bright

with many small, floating lives, and lost nerves,
hanging almost directly into the valuum inside of me,
the fate of ethers to hang this way, into the vacuum inside of me,
into my flushed nowhere cheeks,
just hatched from my small hands,

smeared all over with my own wet light

dissolvingly, inconsolably, albumenescently so.
Through which please, has been spoken, "pineapple-&-tequila,"
in the form of a two-headed voice, mine,
whomsoever and inconsequentially claps my teeth together
to exhale one more faint page

from this small book of sulphur. One more anybody else,
somebody. A being of smoke
inscribes me as erasing, rising: all repeats
as a thing endlessly inside of me, moving my lips,
blinking my empty eyelid,

among other bright, sudden vessels
that occupy the air beside me, other vibrations
of frustrated waking, her wakelessness among these
in the form of a pea-green bomber coat on a stool beside me,
near the hospital where I haven't suffered,

or even been born.

A face worn bluntly into the grandiose defacement.
I've seen this woman before, and her voice
wears her this afternoon, in the form of pink fiberglass —
a clarity that suffers itself to flash off her dead brother's dogtags,
the ones she wears around her neck.

And if hers shall bear the instant
"Hide your money, Sam,"
then I cannot believe these great, blooming
optic lobes that listen
are able to fit inside my blindness, torn whole and sperm-wet,

set against the light that hides itself in my glowing ears.

Hides itself in the liquids that are composing me.
That which fills my shirt, like a stomach, in the form of this
    waiting
for the sugars to heal me into this place
where things overwhelmingly dwell in their awkward
    distribution —
matchboxes on the bar, zippo-lid clicking shut,

a lunchroom clock on the wall: this emptiness
poised against the counter, and the cinched closing in my belly
searched for its little, human finger.
For a draft off the hospital gasworks
to move the door in its metalloid jamb.

The breadcrumb, caught in the craw of my eye,
to give its issue as a flowing down my cheek,
or backwater from the john constantly rushing in the pipes.
Or me, standing in a blur of fluids,
where the wall hid its veins behind tears of oxidization,

sweat from the pipes. Filled, like me, with pink, contaminated
    cotton —
a gauzlet of surplus voices, including hers,
coming across oceans of formaldehyde through which
I suppose your fear learns to live with you
comes, "one more, Ben," comes please, once, I was spoken

in my listening, I moved this way
because of the sounds that were inside me,
Mutilate me into pure sound, or so the song goes,
swimming forth through the spacious,
elongated earlobe they have carved out for me this afternoon,

of blue tube-flicker and noise,
as though the medicated air were just a place for us
to trade our small emissions: hers,
with its brown hair and glasses and red, distended nose.
My thick silences and baby cheeks: her cheeks

soft as old money I've had my fingers on.
Ruptured, shortwave vessels beneath the eyes,

signifying that to see violently was to drink through
to the heart of exactly such a piercing, nurturing moment
as this, when I actually turned to the woman beside me,
to the tiny cheekhairs that catch the light, and glow,
my little ones, my lost moments,

my red-in-the-face-drunk-ones . . .

Do you love me like I was your brother?

"Nope," she's saying, "no screaming babies
in my ward. Pretty much all of them are intubated,
which means they can't make any vocal sounds —"

Which means I can't speak for the vanished asphodels in my face,
these red shadows. Out of the mask of my sleeping,

they bespeak my past: to go forth
drunk at rush-hour in 15 minutes or so.

Wander among other sneakers sewn together by children in
    Jakarta.
Beneath the skeletal overpass dripping with lights.
Open beloward by a trash-can of burning planks,

Young man in the glasses, God bless you.

He that hath but half an eye.
Have fallen into the tunnel of my seeing as I walked past.
An owl's cry released into that corridor of each hollow,
missing face where its body shall follow, each
with our helmet of dogskin, which, after all,

can't be torn off, cocked to one side
and listening for something: the wearing away of the faces
of those who will not be born,
Those for whome the entry to life is foreclosed,
which can't be torn off, and don't quite hear it on her stool —

what I'll leave here behind me,
inside of her broken face, in a room the size of this one,
already exhausted of the place where I stood once,
now, in a forgotten moment, extinguishing the small fires
with my mouth. Begging the light, another jagged,

6:05 glitter ejaculated off the chromework of a passing car,

another aching behind my eyes to tear me forth,
gracefully, into the plastic motion of many vanished hands;
touch the mechanics of this lesion in time, young man,
droplet of what's born and dying simultaneously,
where the waking shall begin.

Into this orphaned room, the sirens
suddenly shriek human, absorb

their 6:06 to emit *wearepassingwepass*
folded among one another and alone, she,
in her bright green orderly smock:

I, in my stretch-polyester oxford
through which humbly, like a bad tip, nevertheless
I submit my small nipples
to be transmitted now into the high-pitched,
human wailing of small flies that hover

in a small emission of exhaust left in the light,
which of them sings sweetest? —

so that I might become the wet-nurse to this room,
even though I'm its baby...

"Baby," she says into her drink, "the machines.
Sometimes I go home, and hear them in my sleep."

In me what is dark (— illumine —) Does she hear it?
That which comes preinstalled with an unborn face
through the membranes of certain foul, dirty mirrors?
Like that one, behind the bottles, emptied
to a face which is the back of my head,

pressed against the wall? (— raise and support —)
A face which is the buzzing of neon bulbs?
Begging, *irradiate where I've been*: behind many chained,
padlocked storefronts like this,
with its pleasure-having-served-yous, and its arguments,

behind which calls: *my face shall be repeated*
through Sector C of this city of dismantled docks,

used condoms floating on the sickened baywaters,
and I too shall be ingested for this,
our only truly unborn instant,
a destiny of unborn action, must be paid for . . .
behind which calls

the sleep, the sleep —

one small instinct to the next
torn out of the mouth of our general pleasure,
a breathing ward I float through.
Out of the mouth of the past, which was now.
Out of the mouth of the passing, which was then,

born within me as a soft, tearing sound.

From a Book of the Dead

CHAP II.

Containing as Much of the Birth of the Foundling as
can be gathered out of the rubbish of antiquity,
which hath been carefully sifted for that purpose; with other
suitable decorations of death, such as tempest, shipwreck
& earthquake; in which, however, is a sun, a moon,
a star & an angel.

So that the passage of air might breathe with me,
once, long ago, if memory serves, his eyes are staring,
his mouth is open, his wings are spread —
                    Poisoned rain that swept his cheeks,
Today was not Yesterday.

                    Speak to me as if he were
the past, blown backwards facing fixedly this disturbance.

For he is dead in his own lifetime,
                              A gentle breeze
through the litter, corrosives of sunlight
dissolving his eyelids;

                    It has got caught in his wings
with such violence that he can no longer close them,
a fetid, corporeal skin of dissolved fibre & soft light
at the moment of his birth,
                    The entrails of what was left.

                              Dust of asbestos
from his dissipating wings.

The dust of many crumbled cities in a forgetful haze.

I watched his infected skin falling

— When the sunlight lays down its pale, pale skin
to the floor, a few yellowed pages from the Industrial Age,

A sweet disfigurement — with similarly small hands...

It is a simple night that soft footsteps
are born. When I face myself in the buckled window panes —
paper mills, blind smokestacks, moon over the penitentiary.
Buried rivers that murmured the lower voltages,

When my government ships its waste to poorer countries
at night,

Bracelets of underworlded blood, the City of Death
& all that; it is a Shining City, my America,

Piling wreckage upon wreckage & hurls it at his small feet;
in the breezeways, in the alleys, the debris grows skyward

Into which cracks of being he falls.

& suddenly his emptiness
no longer ceases to happen where my fingers are not
but a storm is blowing from Paradise,

Blowing him backwards into a crumpled,
human form.

CHAP. IV.

*Concerning Apparitions. That they are not so frequent in places
where the Gospel prevaileth, as in the dark corners of the Earth.*

Once, long ago, I made a neat incision just below the wrist
where I tucked my child away; as orphanhood belongs
to the poor, it healed into a bloodless pocket of skin, a thin,
aluminum quill

No, it was a lockpick I kept there, for often I was called upon
to escape.

& as we marched, they frequently every Day gave the Dead shout which was repeated as many Times as there were Captives, his wife big with Child & delivered on the Road to Canada, which she called Captive;

    Sun, Moon, Turmoil: Bitter & Sweet waters
Under the Earth: River that has no water

Lie down to sleep in the heavens with my prayer —
Trees that were stars planted in the sky:

Asphodel meadow beneath the Earth:
       Softly she walked to her son's body

— Though the grass will shoot from the land, I am not shoots of
grass —

& has only this to say: 'You look different'

42

Dressed in the hair of the deceased as I am,
Waiting to be born!

        *My Father & Mother, that I had never
seen before, were waiting, & ordered me into a House, to sit down
silent. My Mother began to cry for some time, then dried up her
Tears, & received me for her son.*

I was a gift from the hospital, like Typhus.

        *Consisting of blankets, coats, skins, cloth,
powder, lead, shot, & to each a bag of paint for their own life*

I must have had that 'caught in the machinery'
Way of crying,

        *& put a belt of Wampum round my Neck,
instead of the Rope which I had worn 400 miles.*

Where pain sings to excite its radiance in all things,
a green, fluorescent longing that sighs through my bedsheets
in the Birding Hour of violent dreams,

When things hide in their cold forms,

Soft thigh of my humming engrafted to the heater's softness —

Do you remember me? I'm the one who was born
with both eyes open.

*Where the river takes its beginning I was delivered to three
young Men, who said I was their Brother, & commanded me
to dance round the fire Bare-foot, & sing the* Prisoner's *song.
But apprehending my compliance sinful, I determined to persist
in declining it at all Adventures*

        When I write, I write in a room
wherein many have died — these are called the Shining Ones,

who drift through me in a plume of lost hair — reaching out
to the beginnings of each moment —

       Then a Place waſſoon erected to celebrate
Maſſ in, which being ended we all went over the Mouth of a River,
& then ſaw the town, over a greater River which waſ ſtill frozen.

O happy weight shimmering in its hurt now that we're born.
I was startled by an arc of color in the surface of that pond
& it shadowed my face.

Held up into that willowy space in daddy's hands, a green flicker
Above the water, a reflected rainbow, cold watercress,
What smelled like rubbing alcohol.

It's as if both eyes have been sewn open
ſaying you ſhall dance & ſing

Now that my eyes were bleeding green, little shoulder of color
ripped forth from its arc, you are beautiful when alive!
& all was surface.

      I waited till near dark, with no lingering motion,
a very narrow & ſurprizing Eſcape, from a violent Death, a paſſage
being provided for uſ;

Through the back Part of the Houſe, over ſome high Picketſ,
& out of the City, to the River ſide, where it emptieſ itſelf
into the Eaſt end of Lake Ontario & fled!

The second rainbow arcing the first even more throbbingly
wherein my tongue was asleep on the water — a dove's flight
scarred that side of my vision with its thermal signatures,
not cried out but whispered —

      Till a better birth preſented

Ah sweetly famished mornings I rose into the evening pollution,
my hands so radiant I had to hide them!

CHAP VII.

I find the Print of a Man's Naked Foot.

That boy with a blue, hollow chest & blueish hair.

I passed him one night in the breezeway as I died
with the others. Wore my own skin swabbed in nakedness.
Wore my expression blunt as a knee.

I touched him there instead with similarly small hands,
just a slip of a thing,

I kissed him on his thin shoulder-blade I shall anoint . . .

In his sleep he makes small sounds like the spooling
of tiny electrical meters I could never decipher,
hunched beside me on the bed.

In a headdress of diesel fumes in heavy sunlight at dusk
I shimmered & he swaddled me over from head to foot,
bore my own skin to the savage air until I'm cold again.

He says to me: " You're not naked enough "

I disrobed in the saturated tearing of a breeze
that lifted the palm branches.

He says: "You're not naked"

Lifted my torn skin where the soft light had entered me . . .
Disease

With a kind, gentle, oval face, forgive me for believing
in my own death

& we laughed in one long pull on the bed.

He releases a flaming sparrow into my bedroom to break
the stillness, lifts a glass to my lips, the dust on the water
alive with thin blue flames to break my fever,

I held the charred, dead sparrow in my hands, lying
in the middle of the floor in my sleep, I shall ignite you . . .

Waiting for laughter to excite my sleep, laughter
which died a long time ago in the brooding taste
of a cry trembled through my soft temples.

At some point in those heavy, innocent afternoons,
my voice appeared to me as a high-hung, inhuman,
radar effect — radiant symptom buried in a sweet headache
of light, scratch of a pencil on paper of squirrels' feet
on the tin roof, so that I could listen to it, as if my ear
were a long, tunneled space.

& in the small hours when I returned to his poor shoulder
he was gone; pigeons, or squirrels, I don't know which,
in the dark spaces above my head, were nesting in pink
fiberglass insulation, the high-pitched squealing
of many pulleys —

ERRATA

Containing the insides of a Prison

After a while I began to notice lines from my own
poetry on the walls.

Of a Deaf Man in Hull   There's more than life to this
Under whoſe Tongue a ſtone bred

In faint, blue pencil in the corners of rooms
I did not know, after waking into the white-wash.

Poisonous colors   a scent of peach leaves filled the rooms
Not all of fear is veiled desire,

The faintest, bluest writing! I could never decipher
those words:

Later in that room, the darkness sent down a demonchild
in the form of a small, damp breeze against my neck,
sent down to whisper my name —
                              Phosphorescent shapes

never seen below, down,
Spindrift of wet wind & spume,   Sweet, sleeping sickness, You:

Father, I said, I must turn my drowned pen & shaking hand,
We are born into a series of disasters happening long ago

Did I enter the sun when I slept?

'No; the tenderneſs of a Father'ſ Bowelſ,'   This joyful Sight that
He wept! —

                    Cyanogen fires, aniline ridges, faces,
sheets of hair. Did I *live* in this perfectly preserved past,
canned foods from the forties on the shelves?

There was a man that if he did hear the sound of a Bell,
he would immediately die away—

(& wrote these still, innocent moments through my own skin

special Answers of Prayer made in that place   That People
marvelously preserved)

Which yesterday made my voices so colossal & small,

— My hair swept back by a great wind & the original calamity
that caused it, I turn back to the wreckage,

I leaned, pausing there, each voice was slow & fast —

(& slept the sleep that erases all thought.)

FINIS.

At the Greyhound Terminal Requiem

1.

On the platform, I found my tongue to be at once prehistoric.
Terminal, sister, of sunshine that opens 4:20 pm on the cement,

& plastic, if not new, waiting for a bus to pull away, the bus that
    carried me here,
Children at play
In the park across the lot, slowly declining through my ear
Which has become my entire body
In the uncertain requiem,
Of hydraulic brakes aching out their whalesongs of departure,
A small song the passengers will carry with them
To the corners of the demi-monde,
Away from me,
A collapsed, inhuman configuration, a shocked fabric in many
    ears —
Will last
Long after this brief, inconsequential messenger I have become
Has faded,
At least as far as Peoria;

Will hang to the ground as long as the sunshine,
With its blonde, discarded hairs, will last into a blue glow

That decays upward through the trees into dusk across the lot.

2.

When I say   'You, whom the city slept'

When I say   'You, whom I attempt to visit in my sleep'
    I mean —

Dead movement of air through a horse's mane lies on the terminal,
    My tongue flattened to light,
Dead promise of escape, negative of flight lifeless on the cold
    cement.

Negative of wind, slow trace of what your hair was: a soft voice,
    a trace
Of many faces, all of them yours, all of them passing through me,

All of them mine as I follow it into the waiting room,
The ghost trace of my form bending away in the mirror
        That faces another mirror, when I say you —

I mean this large man who lumbers towards me saying
        "I'm afraid," saying "I'm unacceptable, & cold."

I mean 'ghost of children playing,'   Cast through tall windows
                                                overhead
        Ghost of   'Tear me with your softness'

(In whatever bedroom you open your eyes to a massive,
    constricted banging
In the pipes, what's replaced my voice

                            In a room unlike this room —)

Hunched, occupied benches. A vaulted draughty ceiling. Fake
    marble floor.

Lain in lifelessness in a scrap of paper at my feet —

"Would you please give me a copy of the Lord Have Mercy
        We're using at Lent, Dear Fileman?"

(Says —   'I came to you last night in my sleep'

The plaster wing from a child's pageant in my ripped knapsack
The movement in my fingers said   Brokentornplasterrun

When the absolute city slept.   I attempted to touch you.
The movement in my fingers attempted:

                              'Tears open the sky behind my face.'

Each face which, just now, in my sleep, was worn to bluntness,
As in a city like this one, now, here, smothered in the beating

Of police helicopters,

          & your neck as I held it — somehow long, then, in my sleep,
Like a horse's neck.

I saw my face, wrapped around itself & smearing away in a water
     glass
                              On the bedside table.

I felt my face small, worn smooth in your hand as you lifted it
          Petrified Metropolis of crystal.

                         Moving against me like a horse, I held you.
Your breath was hard against my cheek,
                         A small, blue
Immaculate flame in that moment after waking:

Me, lying there, looking up at you, I say,

Like an alcohol flame that leaves the skin cold & without hair,
Small & blue,

Quivered, ran across my stomach   I watched you walk out
    the door

I was running in my sleep, wrapped smooth in your hands
    I ran
As a crippled man must dream of running)

Until a shifting clunk in the pepsi machine startles me
With my finger paused between Mt. Dew & Dr. Pepper,

A message scrawled in black ink on the dollar bill: *Jesus,*
I ran, in a child's hand: *please, Jesus . . .*

3.
Only to wake now in the voice over the P.A.
5:15 — 6:25 — 11:20

A man's wooden voice worn to bluntness
By the caressing of many hands, announces

Carbondale, Illinois, departing at 5:15
Detroit, 6:25, announces that a little girl's sleeping face,

Carried in the arms of her teenage mom,
Will be passing through me,

With its low, famished voltage,
What's left of your voice, hundreds of miles

Away, the closed eyelids saying, Cleveland,

Indianapolis, Iowa City, a place —
Like the bruises in the hollows of my arms —

Where I can be forgotten,
Destination Unborn, a city, like this one,

Where I wait for a second bus
To carry me away

To another station where I'll stand
Before another vending machine,

Another can of exhaust delivered into my hand,
Where a man's voice announces that to speak

In a place like this
Is to be as inescapable as laughter

In what was once the hour of prayer,
That he who listens hard does not see.

4.
Early this morning, across the aisle from that woman, her girl
    asleep,
The other four passengers asleep, & me, asleep,
She must have heard your voice
Muttered out of my mouth into the cold air
Against my cheek, your voice was real
Through the jammed-open,
Sliding window, it slapped my cheek softly
'I'm cold. I'm always cold,' she must have heard
Before I opened my eyes
& realized where I was, riding in a bus
Through what was once prairie,
Nebraska, maybe, or Kansas, a blue decay
Out of the mouth of clarity — your invisible mouth —
On the decay-line of the sky
Swallowing jagged bits of stars
One by one.

5.

Announces that everything is alive —
Uncertain light of childplay beyond me,

& I am born again as I wander outside once more
Only to stand here on the terminal

As that woman's bus pulls away,
Carrying her little girl, carrying my empty seat in its belly,

Across the aisle from where, I'm cold,
Finds its way through the child's mouth, hush,

Consumed in the buzz
Of the overhead light, diesel fumes, nausea,

The sounds she'll make in her sleep,
A large man shifting in his plastic seat

Ahead of them, empty seats
Shifting with the engine,

& those small, plastic pieces of your voice,
Carried with them vibrating away into the hunger

Of many small, darkened kitchens.

PART THREE

Theories of Color—A Dialogue in the Rainbow

for Sarah Van Wyhe

Methyl violet: a chip of aluminum missing from my cheek.

Today my name was aspir:
Rainbows do not visit the air   violet   *they irradiate it*

The woman swallowing her hair says so
enkindling my fog . . .

Spanning this plastic, aspiring place where your sister was
   murdered.

Methyl violet: the shape of her thigh, a cut of meat.
Methyl violet: my mouth entering the softening of a breeze

Methyl: *my face, thou shalt not see*   so empty, & human,
   & blue.

Crumbling vermicides of sulfur: her vast, mild forehead,
infect & trouble this bible-trice of sight.

Sulfur: crouched above us for days now.
Sulfur: eaten in a birth of color,

as I looked upon the sky, a human breeze visited me: tenderest
   leaf:
Green: a page like this one, lifted in a darkening

through my closed ear: Less green: *"we're not going to injure*
   you" : lest

<u>Red</u>:   I stood in the doorway of its falling, tasted the tiny blood-
   slippers dissolve

Red: these vibrations will not feed us

Red: it has splintered the roots of my hair with regard to life,
       a little to her left. You could almost have touched her in
       those handfuls of hair

Red: but her shoulder backed off, shimmered into a band of
          colors
       & the particles hanged in me, a thousand miles away from
          you

Red: if that was the shadow of a cheekbone in its brutal arc
          then it fell, and falling, tore into the shadows of horse-flesh,

an albescence   *for bloodletting*   where light tears itself to pieces, in-
fusoria of blue: a chip of paint from a blue van

they lifted from under the sole of her shoe with a pair of tweezers,
placed it into a tiny, plastic bag:

Blue: It's then that I remembered how generous the air was
Blue: Torn in the eyes of her toddler.

Onely the briefest waves shall pass through

Beyond   Palest Blue: a painted hunger
The concrescent skies

Blue: hurt through me.

"Colors Are the Deeds of Light, What It Does and What It Suffers"

for Laura Van Wyhe, October 23, 1975–October 26, 1996

And the trees are sudden tonight
In their imitation of your missing hair, brutally sudden,
Sister, evacuated into this turning on the bed,
Appended to my side: this empty, empty color
Of water poured through me into the sound of leaves,
Reaching me from rooms ago:
You were standing there, above, 8 months pregnant,
The pale-blue in your eye having swallowed my face,
Coated those small, distorted cheeks in the birth of an animal color
— The inner lining of that touch —
Your pregnant stomach against my upper arm.
I was holding a child's drawing of a rainbow, scribbled in crayon.
And your hair fell over my face as you leaned down to pull open the curtain:
Between the organ of my blindness, and the organ of this silence,
In which I float tonight as an upside down image,
Newly awakened, into the flutter of white moths
Against the window-pane,
It was released behind a swathe of sunlight,
Pages and pages of it, a missing color cast through you
In the direction of my apparent movement: *into* your eye,
Towards the pale-blue corner reflected there, rounded away at the
    side:
Drawn back, emptied through that glassy,
Placental little room in your eye,
Where the light bends away, discarding its faces,

Into a place like this, as one of the small, violet palpitations
This moment sheds through its long, naked, fluorescent tube
    on the wall,
Against the skin on my stomach now, into my eyes,
A measure of your missing particles,
And that color, they cast through you then from that room
Into this one, to wake me, as one of these
Moths, hungering at the windowpane;
Those degraded, purple underfringes they fade into
When I shift my gaze, and let it float across the plaster wall,
As though they too could reverse themselves
Through the ghostly, nervous flight of their images
And feed off the warmth between us,
What has fallen in between these two rooms, and emerged
    within *me*,
That which takes its color as my turning on the mattress,
Waking into one of the many incarnations
Of this room, to hold my forehead in my hands:
And feel, with my entire blindness, a trail of wept,
Unknowable colors you released, passing across the surface of
    this waking:
Hey, if you don't watch out, they'll wake you,
But that's impossible, as colors are, when we're asleep.
Then you'll have to bear the throb of this lamp,
Like a thing in pain, that which takes its crying
From the song of a katydid, as I am bearing these small scars
Transmitted through me — flicker, moth, blue of your face —
The ones left behind on each moment as we open
To let it pass through us
On the way to the next plaster, breathing chamber
Where I'll be waiting for you to speak through me,

A blank sheet of paper in my hand, to give back
That part of me which collapsed,
Wildly, inconsolably, inside the shape of that touch:
And its reflection, staring into and out of your eye,
Gone out forever in that emission from my mouth,
That tiny, blue bubble of light, poised on my distorted lips,
A still-point to which my forehead has distended.
As though it might be pulled through
Along with those low plaster ceilings, and the broken television
The pampas grass that stood in the corner,
To look through your murdered, prismatic gaze,
And be born through it — what surrounds me now,
The color of everything and nothing combined,
You'd be looking through it in a month,
Just after he'd crushed your forehead;
This invisible, pale-blueish absence, sister, into which I've
    awakened —
What your eye was — obliquely, shyly, it comes
From behind each object, wall, hand, human heart,
Black glass of the window pane, each a different birth
And shade of blue to this deed:
That the color released from your eyes in that room
Be blocked forever by these scarred surfaces,
Including my flesh, the silent undercolor
And birth-lining of the objects in this room,
Leaving me here, again, again, now,
To beg for your living face to reverse itself through me,
As if my heart were retinal, and your absence, just an image
Rather than an emptiness that impregnates me,
With the shape of your body constantly emptying
Through this dioptric space where I'm lying,

Smothered in that blue blindness delivered through your eye,
And in this moment, the afterbirth of that touch.

Waterfowl Descending

Shall speak to me in their fattening echo, & purr: penetralia,
& the moaning —

The meadow darkens quietly: "the sleep of reason."
My weight: a transponder that looms, spindle & truss, all that
   I was

flashing once from the standing water, & white.

In the tall grass I have an exceptionally long neck, blueish
& metallic in its sheen.

The one brushing a surface with his broken wing, without
   wings.
The one unable to ask.

In the grasses I flick my eyes open like an iguana about to
   suckle . . .

Suckles my injured, reflected hair when I kneel in the water.
Desiccates me cold, a pygmy ravishing an orange.

For those of us who have sinned, pray for us,
I am bathed in a thinner sky, pray for me, each soft,

empty landing a report of my dying now, a backbeat.

(Report: the wind manages to get through me,)

Unfathered, unencrypted through the air, gasoline transpyring.
For those of us who breathe, put your ear

splendidly & cheaply to the ground as they fluster,
imitation parrotmeat, & a bronze feather that falls: my cheeks

flushed, "like the sky at dawn,"

when tall colors reach heavenward, & sicken,
& die —

        Once, I drew a picture
of fowl abreast a hillside, a simple injury, I was a little girl

laughing in the dark, my sylph. These

swift, flicking motions — precisely now — they are beading me
with her small eyes,

& the air sparkles with prerecorded applause,
a delicate weft into the sky, unspooling & saccadic. An

orphan-bird, (a cylinder) of many
colorful sounds I could not decipher, its slick feathers

as of spunne glass to a red throte,

(revolving in my chest when soft thérmidés die —)

shall sicken just back of the ear (& dyed): I heard
what voices we must have been, hlanc, & slender,

hugging the ground when they traveled: hunger,

I am worth my weight in horsemeat.

(Debride: "only the wind shall light your hair on fire,")

onely the grass get through me
who have preyen.

(— aftermath: a second growth of grass in a season —)

They were coming down to visit me when the air parts,
They were lacerating my throte & hungry

(when soft voices die)

into dozens of wishing wings.

"And of the Nature of the Sea Which in Ebbing and Flowing Seemes to Observe so Just a Dance, and Yet Understands No Musicke"

A Song of the Drowned

Into the voice of the dead girl pulled out of me.

Drink the forgotten recently afraid.
Drink of my face beneath th'unbroken nervure.

Of we, who provided new bodies (softer), which bore me
Drink of the impure gazes: If we had lips (soft), to speak:

They swirl around my ankles benumbing them,

Grown out of the cold foam which bore me stand.

At what angle to the slanted rain.

Waves break at my feet among pebbles, shells.
Where the sun hid itself among sea-waste: glazed branches,
    strings of jelly
And the sea rang each of its tiny, missing bells in my inner ear.

Roaring its rasures through my eyelids —
Thrall to the sea: the form
Of liquified perukes
That I might lift my hair (the eyes torn in me) and baldheaded,

Bow to the sea in a moment of prayer,

They shawl me as under a black, clear tongue immaculate,

The still unmoving dead

Full of medical waste.
Where my heart would be, in this,
A Thule hour, where the poisoning began in me,

A drownedspace to fill. Hearthanged around my neck.

I was born to sound: a voice forgotten its body.
Among those who drowned here was a young pregnant woman,

Flashed at my feet when she broke
Among silvers of annihilated wheat.

Oombed here in your green speaking curled

Into the underbelly of a wave,

Into its cavernous little girl's voice:

(Speak for the abandoned in their shining path of least:)
Blotted out where they took my neck apart at the nape.

Clamoring through these indefinite ribcages,

Through bodies of missing light.
Scrawled, tossed down on broke-backed waves

At what angle to the dys solved mother I carry within me

A portal of mere standing foam. Opening, swallowing, sobbing,
O breast within to consume a newborn throbbing in my chest.

In polluted, holy, insensate pages of sea-marrow
With your many Sabbaths spilled through my toes.

Tossed heavily on decapitating spokes the water
Has rendered
Into white maresilk, in this manner, moan Sea-she,

With flamelike motions of dauncing
Where the sun hid its pale, reflection. Call to your sperme,

That I might finish myself in thee.

I know the hunger behind my face,
Smeared with human light,
Released above me into pieces of dirty white torn away

With a cry, a cry...

A garbage sifting gull cut a wide swathe
In the air above where I was.

Spilling its birthabsences away into the sky,

To be born over and over, away, then swooping back down,
With a cry torn from my throat,
Cut a wide swathe through me.
The one with tinsel in her beak, flashed to me a signal of the
    drowned:

Rise of this heavy, smokd bodysleep
Formd to fly. Some face

Was trying to be born in me.
Some face my hunger has brought here —

Scrolling through its moments of frightened shilldren.
Its screaming, its silent silver screaming
Lashed to my own spine, thrown down in a hooping motion:

Thole: cast ounds of it down

Which in ebbing and flowing seemes to observe

One day, one day when I stand missing at the sea's edge,
So just a dance: letfall, let   all

Into the hour of erased faces
Suck of her drowned flesh.

Her Blue Dress

A Song of *The Bacchae*

1.

I rose from & pulling your sister's housedress.

What do you bid me seek there raise me thine eyes

Buried in that rayon sky
A fraying apart where it begins.

I watched you replaced by dustfulness composed mostly of light.

That looks through my skin of things that die

& therefore I have veiled my godhead in this wan form,
many soft fingers decaying through the window

into little taps & swatches

its hushed, occipital lobe   pieces of silence
I feel *behind* the light, its

human touching   lifted through sound

small, distant sirens, your voice

finding me to where things sleep —

2.

& took the first, small moment of its tearing

torn tremblingly from the loose, draughty thighs of air

For her heart was dying in the white heart of the fire
& knit into God's flesh

I was not ready to be born

Blue breezes keening through my emptiness

& godhead of its sewn garment called
Di — Wo — Ni — So — Jo

O fragment of the world encircling fire He rent apart

the loom & weaving for an unborn life's desire

yea, his own flesh tore to hide him waiting there to begin

as a dead thing, softly —

3.

Or just fabric.

Heliacal in my lean through that blue sunshine I rose

the small seams tearing around my shoulders
radiant nerve endings

Many violent & innocent deaths I have lived

O blue lips that abbraise me   (your voice)

& pulling those dark rooms ago

a thrushed, sciatic keening   Now — Then

the river that is also an animal
in its still breeze through the pane

Shall I array thee a rich & trailing robe of fine linen

A woman's falling to thy feet

To such a great longing   & rose from the bed

A long tress dangling low beneath thy shoulders

Glistering darkly in & among

Enters me in the form of a blue dress

Over my dark, my heliotropic sex

emptied & poor   to a blue color of immersed flesh

Into feeling it disintegrates against my soft slender

For things of dust   through my empty, human mouth

where your body had been —

4.

Please stop smelling its uprootedness of fresh basil & sex

(I take it against my skin)

A loose weave & threadbare now covers my face, my shoulders

O blue room   my flesh has abandoned
& fray me into many small colors on the sheets

emptied ceaselessly of my dark
through this blue incandescence

(I take your thumbs into my eyesockets)

for this naked turning on the bed, this perishing into nape & arms

its rainbow gardens of the lady

a white, angry fabric   that tore into red & blue

& gentleness through my dead, empty eyes.

5.

Even the corners are unborn   *Life is such a little thing*

Sweetly & forgetfully the rooms fall through me

The human corridors that empty — your hair

disrobing in my face, its soft speaking

Of blue dresses falling to the floor

Listlessly my skin, you pass it through me pale & dressingly

Smothers my mouth in blue clay

Your hair imbibing this drowsy light

Pulls through my blue clay the souls of its smothered falling

I beautifully discard   I take against my skin

each of the naked rooms I have known

6.

                              Round his left arm she put
both hands, set hard against his side her foot,
Drew . . . and the shoulder severed — Not by might
of arm, but easily a red rain fell from the deep green pines
& the trees awoke & knew him —

7.

I have a slender dress.

Disintegrating now into your universe of human dust
               (my soul expands)
Take *this* then, & pull it apart this rainbow gleaning
               (my dress grows heavy)

& digested into our heavy eyesight that kept falling apart

I have a thin dress mostly composed of flesh

(glossolalia   blue arrest)

Hangs in its radiant tatters the thin conflation of my life
                    (my small rooms buried in the air)

That are really just the spaces between each second

waiting to be joined, ripped free

& falling into my blue, my fluent inner thigh —

At the Fairgrounds

Because my future self lies beside a shadow,

because the dawn shadows are rinsing these barbed wire baales.

(O townlights, massacring the vistas of air, I was twelve,
wet from the showers: a big man: a man named
   Moose)

Because the earth remains jagged & broken

to him or her who remains jagged & broken, the world grows

large. By the chained stalls, fifty feet from the river, within earshot,

(his hands soft, & cold)   I waited, my ear pressed to a plank.
(Lock, stock, & barter)   he pulls down on me —

'who could you please with that' America,   my tiny bell,
my broken, ropeladder spine   I'm *his* breath now.

Tongue in my cheek because my name has me chained
(There was no kiss —) to a parking lot

(Then why this penny on my tongue)   Because your kiss

is a puddle, & I'm lying back into the bankrupt sky, who could we
please Moose

I've been swallowing gasoline,
my filthy angels all tanked up — like stolen fire, the sky begins to
   burn,

taking my eye for a grain of salt.
I am, your eyes, like shards, are, the tiny victims

of windshields, they glitter all around me.

(There will be no more kisses   Then why breathe)

2.
Now the sun doesn't tick, or set.
You break open a green stalk: a milkdrop
bleeds onto my thumping wrist
& the river thinks *fire* —
we're all just sliders anyway,
& the river goes on aching by at our feet,
chained in place, stepping into the current, set free twice,
so long, so long,
we'll never be the same,
tinfoil, a leaf carried away,
a stone, crumbling into soil between my fingers,
a concrete island that floats,
maybe a hip once, we eased into a valley of water, please,
& touch the air, a fingerprint,
grooved & dirty, a fingerprint to my waist,
shocked through & drifting, or else, air,
wash ourselves from this bruised skin,
the air looking through *us*, air,
kiss my throat again,
your shadow is a kiss I'm holding,
palm on my stomach,
a breath breaking open,
touches us & sets itself free a dozen times,
here, here, here,
these soaked milkweed feathers that drift
into a tongue:

Song of the Daughter

In my dreams night closes its dirty waters
around the apartment complex.
Your keys strike each other.
They clatter like unoiled machinery,
your cheeks coarse with iron-filings.
When I lift the dogwood blossom out of water
and glass, dripping with the only light
in the room, it grows immense, deepens,
white as milk around me, a fly
crouched on the pistil.

Father, when I was a girl,
you'd walk from the den at night,
the floorboards creaking like a thousand rusty hinges
flying open. You'd stand in my room,
in the muted flicker of the television,
a blue deep as the light thrown
from water. And then your zipper,
a sewn wound popping open, stitch by stitch, the flies
swarming from their nest, armpit, crotch. Even now
they glitter like scales, blue and green
in the streetlamp. Even now your tongue
slips, slow as the blossom from its sheath,
your arms, your hips, again, then again
and again and again until I am filled,
I am the red clay after a flood
I am the words trying to say *father*

Tonight I've been taken by the blossoms.
I float here like a burned child
in their blooming solution, here,
in the organic dark, root and bruised petal, leaf,
all joined in the drawing of water.
You are wading in from the doorway, neck-deep
and silent, brushing aside the fish,
the drifting weeds, your black chemicals
swallow me, swallow me.

Everlasting Quail

Then the air was a brutal architecture of sugar.

Boys wading to their knees
into blue carpeting,

centurions at dawn, waist-deep in the street
& drunk, looking for her —

Meanwhile the cherry tree was dripping with bees,
a tremble of everlasting quail . . .

I left my wife in a tall hotel.

Wasn't that the room where they grew bigger trees?
There were tall buildings darkening in the clouds.

(Human: I must have been an enormous bishop
swinging a silver teaball in the kitchen.)

And today, a day so peaceful & sunny-side up,
a day for being alive.

The day I am scheduled to lose my mouth?
Everybody has spoken through this throat:

"I don't think in the end God wishes us to be human"
where money lies down on the floor.

She was a smudged photo of sleep, her blonde
empty cheeks faceless & streaming.

I dropped a coin into her mouth
and walked off.

(At night I repeat the word 'pillow.'

Pillow: a naked footstep slapping the pavement.
Orphan: the wind that eats my laughing chest,)

empty: my laughing chest: my cheeks.

Notes

PART I

Epigraph: From *Introducing Walter Benjamin,* by Howard Caygill, Alex Coles, Andrzej Klimowski, with Richard Appignanesi (Totem Books, 1998).

"Zeromass/*Erozmass*": The poem is intended to be read in the traditional fashion, left to right, down the page.

"Michael Masse": Michaelmas is the feast of the archangel Michael, a church festival celebrated on September 29 and one of the four quarter days in England.

"Beverley": This poem, as well as "The Nap" and "Zeromass/*Erozmass*," are dedicated to Beverley Crenshaw and Sally Crenshaw Witt. The final couplet is taken from "The Dream of a Ridiculous Man," by Fyodor Dostoevsky.

"Americana 1": "*Speake, Sister, that I may know thee . . .*" is a line from a play by Ben Jonson. The description of the comet has a real source — the Hale-Bopp comet, which was visible from my apartment on Eureka Street in San Francisco in March 1997 — and a literary one — the description of a prophetic comet in *A Journal of the Plague Year* (1722), by Daniel Defoe.

"Americana 2": "*And through thee, mother, darkness hath fallen on my eyes*" is adapted from *Oedipus Rex,* by Sophocles (c. 406 B.C.).

"The Fine Art of the Skull": This title was stolen verbatim from the cover of a copy of *Ranger Rick.* Some of the italicized lines were reconstructed from *Moby-Dick,* (1851), by Herman Melville.

PART II

"A Face at the Hospital Bar": Line 116: "That therefore which the Scripture cleerely sheweth, we say that God by eternall and unchangeable counsell hath once appointed whome in time to come he would take to salvation, and on the other side whome he would condemne to destruction. This counsell as touching the elect, wee say to bee grounded uponn his free mercie without any respect of the worthiness of man, but whome hee appointeth to damnation, to them by his just in deed and irreprehensible, but also incomprehensible judgment, *the entry of life is foreclosed.*" John Calvin, *Horribile Decretum.*

Line 140: "For els to thinke that those powers (if there be any such) above, are moved either by the eloquence of our prayers, or in a chafe by the folly of our actions; carries as much reason as if flies should thinke, that men take great care *which of them hums sweetest,* and which of them flies nimblest." *Arcadia* (c. 1580; pub. 1590), by Sir Philip Sidney.

Lines 155-164: Phrases from the invocation of *Paradise Lost* (1667), by John Milton are woven into these lines.

"From a Book of the Dead": The Arguments for each chapter were composed from a variety of different sources, including: *Candide* (1759), by Voltaire; *Tom Jones* (1749), and *Jonathon Wild* (1743), by Henry Fielding; *An Essay for the Recording of Illustrious Providences,* by Increase Mather; *The Captivity of Robert Eastburn,* by Robert Eastburn; and *Robinson Crusoe,* (1719–1720), by Daniel Defoe.

"Chapter II": Walter Benjamin's passage on the Angel of History, part IX of the essay "Theses on the Philosophy of History," was an important starting point for this section:

> A Klee painting named "Angelus Novus" shows an angel looking as though he is about to move away from something he is fixedly contemplating. His eyes are staring, his mouth is open, his wings are spread. This is how one pictures the angel of history. His face is turned towards the past. Where we perceive a chain of events, he sees one single catastrophe which keeps piling wreckage upon wreckage and hurls it in front of his feet. The angel would like to stay, awaken the dead, and make whole what has been smashed. But a storm is blowing from Paradise; it has got caught in his wings with such violence that the angel can no longer close them. This storm irresistibly propels him into the future to which his back is turned, while the pile of debris before him grows skyward. This storm is what we call progress.

The passage is from *Illuminations*, by Walter Benjamin (1892–1940), ed. by Hannah Arendt, transl. by Harry Zohn; Harcourt, Brace, Jovanovich, 1968.

"Chapter VII": Sources for this chapter include *Poems of Heaven and Hell from Ancient Mesopotomia*, ed. and trans. by N. K. Sandars, (The Penguin Group, Viking Penguin Inc., 1971), especially "The Babylonian Creation," "The Sumerian Underworld," "Inanna's Journey to Hell," and Sandar's introduction. Italicized passages were sampled from *The Captivity Narrative of Robert Eastburn* and recomposed to suit the purposes of the poem. Thanks to Chris Adrian.

"At the Greyhound Terminal Bus Requiem": The phrase "tears open the sky behind my face" is adapted from a line from the essay "Franz Kafka," by Walter Benjamin. The last line of section three ("he who listens hard does not see") was taken verbatim from an essay entitled "Some reflections on Kafka," also by Benjamin, in *Illuminations*.

PART III

"Theories of Color" : The italicized lines at the beginning are bits and pieces stitched together from *Moby-Dick* (1851), by Herman Melville.

"Colors Are the Deeds of Light, What It Does and What It Suffers": The title is taken from the introduction to *Theory of Color* (1808), by Johann Wolfgang von Goethe, from *Scientific Studies by Johann Wolfgang von Goethe*, ed. and trans. by Douglas Miller (Princeton University Press, 1995). Miller, however, translates the word "suffer" as "endures."

"Waterfowl Descending": "The sleep of reason," as well as the poem itself, is adapted from an etching by Francisco Jose de Goya y Lucientes, entitled "The Dream of Reason." About this etching Goya once wrote, "the dream of reason engenders monsters." Certain lines are taken from various religious ceremonies; for example, "the one unable to ask," is part of the Passover Seder. "When soft voices die" is from a lyric by Percy Bysshe Shelley, entitled "TO ——", (1821).

"And of the Nature of the Sea Which in Ebbing and Flowing Seemes to Observe so Just a Dance, and yet Understands No Musicke" The title of this poem was lifted verbatim from *Arcadia* (c. 1580; pub. 1590), by Sir Philip Sidney.

"Her Blue Dress": The poem relies heavily on a knowledge of the play *The Bacchae*, by Euripides (c. 405 B.C.) as well as variations on the myth of Dionysus' birth; some of its lines, in sections 1, 2, and especially 5, were composed by piecing together random phrases and images from Gilbert Murray's 1938 translation of the play (Random House, 1938). The speaker is a lyric amalgam of, among other things, Pentheus (which suggests penthos, or sorrow), Dionysus, Agave (the mother of Pentheus), and a contemporary male speaker who, like the King of Thebes, steps into a woman's clothing so as to witness something forbidden to him and transforms himself in the process. Gratitude is offered to Lynn and Bill Define for giving me the Murray translation, and of course to D. A. Powell, who helped me make use of it.

"Everlasting Quail": The title was lifted from the name of a Chinese restaurant in San Francisco. There also happens to be a company that produces a line of quail eggs entitled "Neverending Quail."